Spring Tea

a celebration of grace and courtesy

for children three to six

Linda Seeley, Alison Ney & Cameron Sesto

Master Class Materials

Linda Seeley — *Creator of the Spring Tea, Montessori Teacher and Teacher Trainer*
Alison Ney — *Author, Photographer, Montessori Teacher*
Kindergarten Students at Stoneridge Montessori School — *Illustrations*
Cameron Sesto — *Design, Production, Visual Recipes, Montessori Art Teacher*

Table of Contents

Introduction

One of my fondest childhood memories was having tea parties with my grandmother. She was a wonderful Victorian lady who delighted in using her best china while sharing ceremonies, rituals, and celebrations with her granddaughter. Many of these tea parties were associated with the seasons: Summer Teas with fresh strawberries, the first days of winter by the fire and probably most memorable, Spring Teas.

Once married with children of my own, I endeavored to replicate these teas with my daughters. Later, as a Montessori teacher, I decided to have Spring Teas with my class. I have now participated in over 30 Spring Teas, each one a unique and memorable event. Finding Spring Tea to be so memorable for both parents and children, I was encouraged by close friends and colleagues, Alison and Cameron, to collaborate on creating a guide for classroom tea parties so that many more adults and children can share this delightful tradition.

Many cultures around the world stop for tea. It is a time to slow down, talk with one another, and renew the spirit. For children it can be a time to teach life skills, manners, and socialization. We know that ritual and routine create a rhythm in the lives of children. With an annual classroom tea, they get to look forward in time and think about something to give, rather than receive. It helps to develop the very important resiliency skill of waiting. Learning to wait is even more important these days when immediate gratification is the norm rather than the exception. The annual tradition creates an opportunity for reflection on the past, bringing it into the present and projecting it to the future.

There is such pride for children who get to host a guest, serve food that they have prepared and then be trusted to carry the beautiful, fragile teacup. Shared social experiences follow. Children learn to chat and make polite conversation. They feel the empowerment of saying, *please, thank you*, and *may I get you some more*? The children feel affirmed!

The Spring Tea provides an opportunity for the guests (usually parents) to make time for the children and to remind the children of the important place they hold in the guests' hearts. The classroom tea truly belongs to the children. They did it, they made it, and they carry it out—authentically, not artificially. Children who learn and practice kindness and gratitude will find social situations elsewhere and in their later lives instinctively easier. As classroom teachers we get to experience the community of the classroom and to celebrate the growth of the children. I hope you find this guide helpful and inspiring.

Have a cup of tea and be ready to create memories!

Linda Seeley

Linda Seeley
Ipswich, MA 2011

Preparations: Work of the Adult

Announcements and Invitations

Once you have decided to have a spring tea it is important to add it to the school's master calendar as soon as possible – preferably at the start of the new school year. Consider mentioning your intention to have a spring tea to parents during orientation or welcome back meetings so they can plan for it later in the year.

Approximately two to three weeks prior to the date of the tea, send home an announcement letting everyone know about the tea and what to expect. Details should include who is invited, what refreshments will be served, the date, time, and location of the tea(s), and suggested attire. We have included a sample letter in our Templates pages.

Child-created invitations can be prepared during class time and sent home one to two weeks prior to the tea. If using our teacup template, we recommend that the adult cut out the teacups after they are decorated to ensure that none of the inside wording is cut away inadvertently. The adult can also cut the slit in the "tea" for the R.S.V.P. form and string the teabags through the opening. (See photo below.)

Preparations: Work of the Child

Announcements and Invitations

Each child creates a special invitation for his/her guest(s). We suggest a *tea-themed* invitation such as the teacup shaped template included in the Templates pages. Children can use paint, markers, crayons, daubers, collage, or whatever you have on hand to decorate the outside of each invitation. On the inside, cards should be printed with the details of the tea including date, time, and location. There should be enough space left for the child to sign his/her name at the bottom.

Be sure to include instructions for the R.S.V.P. With the teacup template, we used a "tea bag" on a ribbon that could be inserted into a slit in the card. A heart-shaped tag hangs from the outside of the card. Inside, there is space for guests to write their name(s) and the name of the child. Our tradition is to return each completed teabag to a special teapot set up outside the classroom.

Preparations: Work of the Adult

The Menu

The menu can be set at any time, but we recommend brainstorming ideas and locating recipes at least four to six weeks prior to the tea. This will allow you time to make shopping lists and set a comfortable baking schedule for the classroom. Some tea treats can be made in advance and frozen until it's time for the tea.

When setting the menu, take into account how much baking experience the classroom has as well as the culture of your school. Tea menus can be simple or elaborate depending on expectations and time. We have found that too many choices can be overwhelming for both children and adults, so have settled on a combination of baked goods, sandwiches, and fruit that works for our classrooms.

The favorite and most anticipated treat for our teas is cucumber sandwiches. These are made either the afternoon before or the morning of the tea to ensure crunchy cucumbers and firm bread. Other menu items have included baked goods like cut-out sugar cookies, small tarts or scones, tea breads, bite-sized brownies, and fruits such as whole strawberries or mixed fruit kabobs with chunks of cheese. We have found that small snacks that can be eaten with your fingers work best and minimize the use of cutlery. A list of our most successful menu items is included in the Suggestions pages.

Once the menu is set, you may want to create a menu card to place at each table setting. This card lists the treats available at the serving table and offers the child and his/her guest an opportunity to discuss what they will eat before going to the serving table to choose something! A sample menu card is included in the Templates pages.

Just as important as your treat menu is your choice of beverages! For adults we offer fine British tea. You can find affordable and delicious English tea in the international section of most major grocery stores. Other options may include your favorite brand of tea, herbal teas, or coffee. Whatever your choice, be sure to have milk, sugar, honey, and lemon on hand for the day of the tea so the guests can drink their tea as they prefer it.

For the children, we suggest cold, non-caffeinated options like pink lemonade or water. However, you could consider including herbal teas or iced teas as an option. Offering just one or two choices will help make serving quick and efficient.

Finally, we suggest creating a beverage order form for children to fill out while sitting with their guests. This form includes options for tea, milk, sugar, honey, and lemon. You will find a sample in the Suggestions pages.

Preparations: Work of the Child

Baking/Preparing the Food

Once the menu has been set and the ingredients have been purchased, the children can start baking! Child-friendly recipes for two of our best loved tea treats—cucumber sandwiches and strawberry tarts—are included in the following pages.

Recipe 1. Cucumber Sandwiches

Ingredients	**Utensils**
Deli Bread	Plate
Fresh Dill or Italian Seasonings	Mixing Bowl
Bowl of Sliced Cucumbers	Mixing Spoon
Block of Cream Cheese	Spreader

Cucumber Sandwiches
Instructions #1

1. Wash your hands.

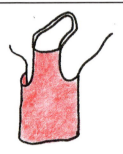

2. Put on an apron.

3. Add the Italian spice mix.

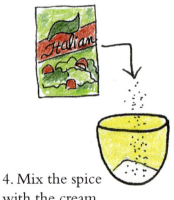

4. Mix the spice with the cream cheese.

5. Put the cream cheese in a mixing bowl.

6. Spread the cream cheese mixture on deli bread.

7. Place a cucumber slice on top of the cream cheese.

8. Arrange the bread on a pretty plate. Add a sprig of fresh dill if you have it.

9. Yum! What a delicious treat!

10. Clean up and wash the dishes.

Recipe 2. The Queen of Hearts Made some Tarts

Ingredients	**Utensils**

 Pie Crust

 Round cookie cutter

 Strawberry Jam

 Timer

Utensils

  Wax Paper

 Oven Mitt

 Fork

 Toaster Oven

 Spoon

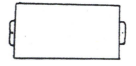 Cookie Sheet

Strawberry Tarts
Instructions #1

1. Wash your hands.

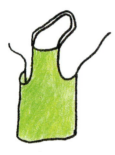

2. Put on an apron.

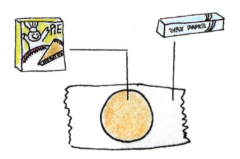

3. Put the pie crust on the wax paper.

4. Cut out round pieces of dough with the cookie cutter.

5. Put a spoonful of strawberry jam in the center of each round.

6. Fold the round in half. Use a fork to press down the edges.

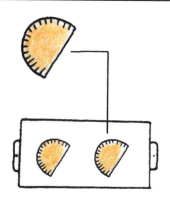

7. Put your tarts on a cookie sheet.

8. Put in the oven at 350 degrees. Bake for 10 minutes.

9. Use an oven mitt to take the cookie sheet out of the oven.

10. When your tarts are cook, put them on a plate.

11. YUM!!

12. Wash the dishes and tidy up.

Preparations: Work of the Adult

Decorations

Depending on where you choose to hold your tea, you may want to have the children create art to decorate the walls or doors. As our teas are held in the spring, we typically have a flower theme to our decorations. These have included hand-printed tulips, flower gardens, and spring portraits of our guests. We are sure to adorn the room with bouquets and pots of garden fresh flowers and plants.

Preparations: Work of the Child

Decorations

It is important to leave enough time both to create any wall decorations and to hang them. Depending on what you choose to create and where you hold your tea, you may be able to hang art a week or two prior to the event. However, you don't want to decorate so early that the beautiful makeover of the tea room is not a surprise to guests and children. Entering the transformed "tea room" on the morning of the event is a moment of awe and wonder to children and should be a wonderful surprise to guests.

Preparations: Work of the Adult

Gifts

Similar to setting the menu, gift ideas can be decided at any time, but we recommend brainstorming ideas and locating materials at least four to six weeks prior to the tea. This will allow ample time to schedule the gift creation for the classroom without feeling rushed. As with treats, gifts can potentially be made in advance and put away until it's time for the tea. We try to have three or four good ideas for gifts that we rotate each year. That way a guest who attends each year doesn't receive any repeat gifts. Successful ideas have included hand painted tiles, magnets, decorated memo clips, and various types of jewelry.

Gift wrapping is optional. However, if you decide to wrap gifts, be sure to include these materials in your initial shopping list and build time into your schedule for children to wrap and label their items.

We suggest making a card to go with the gift. Photographs of the children are a lovely option for the front. They could be candid pictures taken earlier in the year, or might be posed headshots that you take outside of your classroom one sunny, spring day. Cards can contain whatever greeting you like and are signed by each child to the best of his/her ability.

In addition to these gifts, you may choose to create an "interview" booklet for guests to take home as a memento of the tea. These booklets contain brief descriptions of each guest who attends the tea as related by their young hosts. They should have a beautiful, dated cover and might begin with a dedication page created by the child followed by brief interviews. Questions are open-ended, such as "What does your guest do for work?" or "What does your guest like to do to relax?" Answers should be written exactly as dictated by the child and transcribed by an adult. Once you have developed a short questionnaire, be sure to build time into your tea preparation schedule to create a cover and a dedication page as well as time to conduct interviews, type responses, and copy and collate each part of the booklet.

We have found it most efficient for an adult to coordinate this last part of the project. A sample booklet cover and dedication page may be found in the Templates pages. Sample questions and write-ups can be found in the Suggestions pages.

Finally, our school's tradition has included giving a long-stemmed rose to each guest as the tea comes to a close. Roses are passed from an adult to a child and from the child to the guest and indicate that the event is complete. As roses are fragile flowers, we recommend purchasing them the morning of the tea or the evening prior to ensure they are fresh and beautiful.

Please take a moment to review the Suggestions pages for a list of gift ideas.

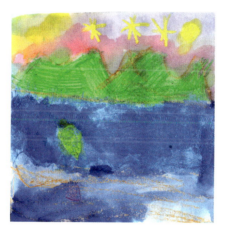

Memo Clips

Calendar

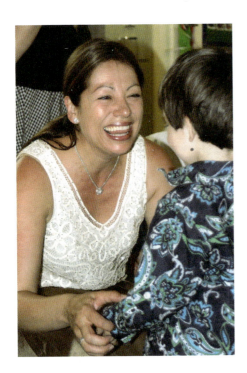

Mussel Pin with beads

Preparations: Work of the Child

Gifts

The children enjoy creating beautiful gifts for their guests. It is especially exciting to keep their special creations secret until the day of the tea. They are proud to present the gifts, cards, and roses to special guests and enjoy listening to their interviews as they are read from the booklets.

Another option for the table is a place card for the guest. When provided with a small "tent" made from construction paper or card stock, the child can write his/her guest's name (Margaret) or nickname ("Mom" or "Grandma"). Place cards can be plain or decorated by the child with stamps, small drawings, or stickers.

Button Pin

Preparations: Work of the Adult

Entertainment

One of the most anticipated moments of the tea is a brief program put on by the children after refreshments. It might include singing, dancing, finger plays, poetry, or even a short skit – whatever the children love to do! To ensure that everyone feels comfortable with words and movement, we suggest choosing material you all know and love, or making sure you begin to practice your program several weeks prior to the tea.

Tea-themed songs and finger plays like "The Teapot Song" or "Cup of Tea" are crowd-pleasing favorites. You might also include a song or two that encourage guests to sing along. Create lyric sheets or choose songs that everyone knows, like "Sing a Song of Sixpence" or "Do You Know the Muffin Man?"

The most important thing to remember is that everyone—children and guests alike—should have fun!

Preparations: Work of the Child

Entertainment

Some of our best-loved programs have included
the following songs and finger plays:

The Teapot Song

I'm a little teapot,

short and stout,

here is my handle (one hand on hip),

here is my spout (other arm out with elbow

and wrist bent).

When I get all steamed up,

hear me shout,

tip me over and pour me out (bend toward spout)!

I'm a special teapot (hand on hip & other arm out).

Yes, it's true.

Here's an example of what I can do.

I can turn my handle into a spout (switch arms),

Tip me over and pour me out (bend toward spout)!

Cup of Tea (fingerplay)

Here's a cup (form a cup by making a loose fist with one hand),

And here's a cup (form a cup with the other hand),

And here's a pot of tea. (Form a pot by pushing both fists together)

Pour a cup, (Use one hand to pretend to pour into the other.)

And pour a cup, (Use the other hand to pretend to pour.)

And have a drink with me. (Pretend to drink.)

Sing a Song of Sixpence (English nursery rhyme)

Sing a song of sixpence,
a pocket full of rye;
four and twenty blackbirds,
baked in a pie.

When the pie was opened,
the birds began to sing;
wasn't that a dainty dish,
to set before the king?

The king was in his counting house,
counting out his money;
the queen was in the parlor,
eating bread and honey.

The maid was in the garden,
hanging out the clothes;
when down came a blackbird,
and took off her nose.

There was such a commotion,
that little Jenny wren
flew down into the garden,
and put it back again!

Grace and Courtesy: Work of the Adult

Lessons in grace and courtesy form the cornerstone of the Montessori Practical Life curriculum. Spring Tea is a celebration of grace and courtesy, giving children an opportunity to use many of the skills they have mastered throughout the year. During the tea, children will greet guests, guide them to their tables, pull out chairs, make polite conversation, take orders, carry teacups and trays, pour drinks, and so much more!

Because the tea includes so many different elements of grace and courtesy, it is important to find ample time during the school day for children to practice. We recommend setting up a small tea table in the classroom where the children can seat a guest, take an order, serve treats, and pour drinks. As with all new materials, children should be given a complete lesson on what is expected when sitting at the table. We usually conduct this in either a full class or small-group lesson format with an adult acting as the guest and another as the child. Once this demonstration has taken place, pairs of children can practice under the guidance of an older child or adult.

Grace and Courtesy: Work of the Child

Children Practice

In the tearoom, tables are set with plates, napkins, two teacups (one large and one small), and a small centerpiece bouquet. An order form and small pencil are on the child's side of the table. A place card, gift, card and program are on the guest's side of the table. Children are seated facing the door to the classroom where their guests will arrive.

At the start of the tea, the lights are low, and an adult greets each guest individually at the door: "Good morning, Mrs. Jones." When Mrs. Jones' guest sees her standing at the door, the child stands up, tucks in his/her chair and walks to the door. The child greets his/her guest: "Good morning, Mom." The child takes the guest's hand, and leads her to her seat. Once at the table, the child pulls out the chair for the guest, seats her, and takes his/her own seat. Children whose guests have arrived stay in their places and make polite conversation until all guests have been seated.

When all guests have arrived and settled in to their seats, the lights come up, giving children the cue that tea time has begun. They may now begin taking beverage orders for their guests. Children should start by writing their names at the bottom of the order forms. They can check off tea with milk or lemon and sugar or honey. Our order form includes two boxes for sugar, so children can ask their guests if they would like one or two spoonfuls of sugar. We also point out that most guests will not choose both sugar and honey.

Once the order form is complete, the child folds it in fourths and places it in the guest's teacup. Next, he or she carries the teacup, saucer, and order form to the serving station, where an adult will fill the order and deliver it to the table.

When giving the lesson on tea, we practice how to hold a teacup and saucer carefully and quietly by holding the handle with a pincer grip and supporting the teacup with the remaining fingers underneath.

Once the children have delivered the teacup and order, they may select a serving tray of treats to take back to their table. Carrying it carefully, the child offers treats to the guest: "Would you care for a treat?" After the guest has been served, the children may choose treats for themselves. After serving, the children return the trays to the serving area so they may be refilled. We allow children to visit the serving table as many times as they'd like during the tea. However, we ask them to take no more than three treats at a time. In this way we hope to reduce waste and not over-indulge in treats!

At the close of the program, traditionally boys bow and girls curtsey, while the guests applaud their performance. We then call the children one by one to take a rose to their guests. This signals the end of the tea.

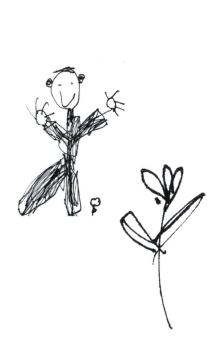

Care of the Environment: Work of the Adult

Setting the Tearoom:

If you have a dedicated space where the tea may be held, preparations can take place a day or two in advance. Our school uses classrooms, transforming them into tearooms on the afternoon prior to the tea.

When using your classroom, the most time-consuming and adult-centric part of the process is clearing out the dining area. We carefully move all of our shelves, furniture, and materials to the edge of the room and hide them beneath white tablecloths. Bulky and hard-to-camouflage items, including area rugs and rocking chairs, are temporarily relocated to another room in the school.

We recommend setting up one table for each child and his/her guest. We have found that the rectangular work tables (3' x 4') from our classrooms work best. Larger tables are used only if there will be more than one guest or child at the table. Each table needs two chairs that can slide under the table neatly. In order to collect enough chairs for all participants, we always borrow chairs from other classrooms.

Our tradition is to seat the youngest children closest to the treat and beverage serving tables so they have the shortest distance to walk with teacups and trays. The oldest participants are seated the furthest away and look forward to their longer walk as a rite of passage.

Once tables are placed, the tea serving station must be set. We recommend using a lovely cloth to cover this table and finding a formal tea service that you can use to serve hot beverages. We have been fortunate that one of the families in our school has allowed us to borrow an antique silver tea service. In order to ensure timely serving of hot beverages, it is useful to have two teapots along with a creamer, a sugar bowl, a bowl for lemon wedges, a small honey pot, small tongs for the lemons, and a quantity of spoons to measure sugar and stir the drinks. We suggest using a coffee urn to brew all of the tea for the event. The urn can heat the water throughout the morning with tea bags added approximately fifteen minutes prior to the guests' arrival. This allows ample time for tea to steep without getting too strong. Once the tea has brewed it is transferred into a smaller pot for serving in a more elegant manner.

Finally, the treat area should be set. This table looks most inviting with a cloth and a beautiful floral centerpiece. We typically use the long-stemmed roses that the children offer their guests as a decoration for the treat table. Small trays containing an assortment of treats are set along the table for children to collect once the tea has begun. An empty classroom shelf is put to use storing extra treats until they are needed to refill serving trays.

We like to ask older children (Upper Elementary or Middle School) and colleagues to assist during the tea. They can help serve tea or lemonade, replenish trays, take photographs, or whatever else may be helpful to make the tea run smoothly.

Care of the Environment: Work of the Child

When the room is clear, children can help pick up any wayward items on the floor and sweep it clean. The older children are delighted to carry and arrange tables and chairs to set the tearoom. It is wonderful, physical work resulting in a pleasantly designed room. When tables are set, the children put their scrubbing skills to work making sure that each table is sparkling clean.

By following a seating chart the children set each place with a plate, teacup, saucer and a napkin. They place an order form and pencil on the child's side and the appropriate place card, menu, gift, card and interview booklet at the guest's place. Every table also receives a small doily and vase of flowers.

Tidying the Tearoom

Once the tea is complete and the last guests have gone, the task of tidying the room and returning it to its original form begins. Tables and chairs must be returned to their places, and the laundry and dishes must be done.

We recommend dividing the tasks between children and adults to make things go smoothly. Our method has been to enlist children to help clear and scrub tables, stack dishes, collect pencils, gather napkins and cloths for laundry, distribute bouquets to brighten classrooms, share leftover treats, and move tables and chairs. The adults oversee this process and have final responsibility for restoring the environment to its original, prepared form.

Suggestions

Menu

 Cucumber sandwiches

 Strawberry tarts

 Italian bonbons

 Sugar cookies

 Scones and jam

 Lemon poppy seed bread

 Brownies

 Meringues

Homemade gifts

 Homemade pins – shell, button, etc.

 Tiles with handprints or fingerprint designs

 Decorated memo clips

 Calendars

 Painted flower pots and bulbs/plants

Sample interview questions

 What is your guest's name?

 I call her/him:

 What does your guest look like?

 What does she/he do for work?

 What does she/he like to do at home?

 What does she/he NOT like to do at home?

 When she/he wants to relax by herself/himself, she/he likes to …

 My favorite thing to do with my guest is:

 How much do you love your guest?

Sample write–up:

Janie:

My guest's name is Judy. I call her Momma. My momma looks like a Judy. She's short and she's a grown woman. For work she goes to school and helps me do things that are tricky. At home she likes to build with me and my blocks. She just doesn't want to clean, clean, clean up the kitchen! When she wants to relax by herself, she looks for me and sometimes we watch shows and sometimes I hug her. My favorite thing to do with her is to hug her. I love my mother this much (arms outstretched)!

Photographs during the tea

Take portraits of children and their guests during the tea and post them outside of the classroom or in the school newsletter after the tea has taken place.

Templates

1. Invitation — page 38

This invitation comes from the adult and should be to sent to guests in a timely fashion, approximately two to three weeks prior to the event. You will need to add the information under the Tea Time heading: *room, time,* and *date* of the event.

2. R.S.V.P. — page 39

Cut and glue the pieces together with a thin ribbon.

3. Child's Invitation — pages 40 and 41

Front and back to copy and position onto card stock to become a folded card that children paint and then give to their special guests.

4. Booklet — pages 42 and 43

Cover and inside dedication. Conduct interviews with each child in the classroom and gather together in this booklet. Staple the pages together at the spine.

5. Treat Menu — page 44

A form to copy or scan to use as your menu card.

6. Beverage Order Form — page 45

A form to copy or scan that the children can use to take tea orders.

Invitation

Dear Special Guest,

Soon wonderful aromas will begin to fill our school as the children prepare for one of the most exciting events of the year, the annual Spring Tea! The tea is the expression of so many of the children's skills—they busily bake refreshments, make gifts and cards, arrange the tea room, and practice grace and courtesy.

This is a very memorable time for you and your child. No siblings or other family members please, because space is very limited. If you are unable to attend this event, please designate another adult to take your place.

Tea Time:

The tea begins promptly at 10:00 a.m. (children should arrive at the usual time). We look forward to welcoming you to this festive occasion!

The Children's House Staff

Hats and gloves are optional!

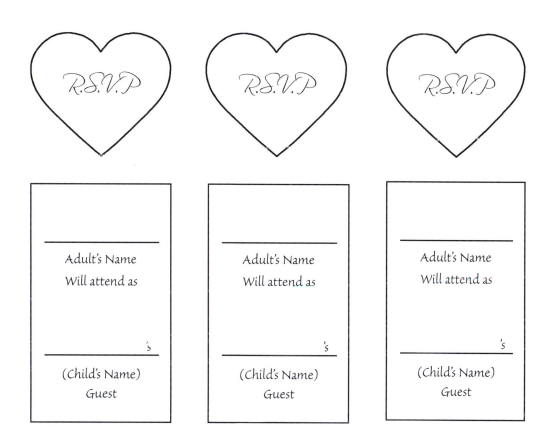

_____

Adult's Name

Will attend as

_____ 's

(Child's Name)

Guest

_____

Adult's Name

Will attend as

_____ 's

(Child's Name)

Guest

_____

Adult's Name

Will attend as

_____ 's

(Child's Name)

Guest

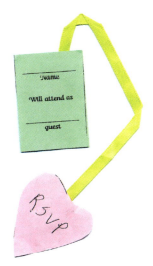

Copy and cut out a heart and card for each child in your classroom. Glue or tape a thin length of ribbon to the back of the heart and attach the other end to the back of the invitation information.

Child's Invitation (outside)

This is the front of the invitation card. Copy the cup so it fits on the **bottom** half of an 8.5 x 11 sheet of white card stock. Each child gets a folded card to decorate as he/she likes.

Please Come to our

Spring Tea

May ___ th ___ am

Please place your tea bag R.S.V.P.
in your classroom teapot.

This is the inside of the invitation card. Place the image upside down on the **top** half of an 8.5 x 11 sheet of white card stock on the reverse side of the paper from the outside invitation so when the card is folded it reads correctly.

Fold the card in half.

Cut out along the teapot outline. (Be sure not to cut the fold at the top of the cup!)

After decorating, children give their folded cards to their special guests.

Spring Tea

When copying, place this image on the right hand side of a full sheet of paper.

This is to be the front of your 5.5 x 8.5 inch booklet containing your write-ups of the children's interviews about their special guests.

Dedicated To:

This is the first inside page of the booklet that contains your write-up of the children's interviews about their guests.

Fold full pages in half and staple the booklet together at the spine so you end up with a booklet that is 8.5 inches high and 5.5 inches wide.

Treat Menu

_____

_____

_____

_____

_____

_____

Copy or scan and fill in the blanks with the food you will be serving on the day of the tea.

My Order

Tea ☐

Milk ☐

Sugar ☐ ☐

Honey ☐

Lemon ☐

Name:_____

Copy or scan the order forms for the children to use to take tea orders.

Planning Time Line

Beginning of School Year (Fall)

Announce plans for Spring Tea in "Back to School Night" meetings.
Add dates to School Master Calendar.

Six to Eight Weeks Prior to Tea

Choose gift and decide whether it will be wrapped or not. Determine materials needed.
Compile shopping list.
Choose songs and/or other entertainment.
Introduce songs, poems, and finger plays as part of weekly music class
or circles.
Choose menu and determine ingredients needed. Compile shopping list.
Put a note in the school newsletter.

Three Weeks Prior to Tea

Send home memo to parents (See Templates pages.)
Make teacup invitation and RSVP templates for the class. (See Templates
pages.)
Compile interview questions and copy questionnaires for each member of
the class. (See Suggestions pages.)
Choose and/or create interview booklet cover and dedication page. (See
Templates pages.)

Two Weeks Prior to Tea

Decide on card design and create them or use photographs.
Make place card templates for the class.
Set up a practice tea table and demonstrate for the class.
Copy black-and-white order forms for practice. (See Templates pages.)
Practice songs or other entertainment daily.
Begin to create room decorations.
Purchase materials for gifts and wrapping.
Begin to conduct interviews.

One Week Prior to Tea

Set up teapot(s) outside of the classroom to receive RSVP teabag cards.
Send home teacup invitations.
Purchase ingredients and begin baking. Create menu items that can be stored
or frozen.
Create menu cards if desired. (See Templates pages.)
Create gifts and wrap them.
Create cards and ask children to add greetings and signatures.

Children write guests' names on place cards.

Children draw portraits of guests for dedication pages.

Type, proof, and print interviews. Compile interview booklets.

Week of Tea

Copy color order forms.

Gather plates, napkins, spoons, serving trays, tea service, coffee urn, pencils, doilies, small vases for tables.

Purchase last-minute menu items (milk, strawberries/fruit, cucumbers, etc.)

Day Prior to Tea

Set up the tea room and hang decorations.

Gather flowers and place throughout the room and on tables.

Arrange gifts, interview booklets, cards, place cards, menu cards, and order forms at each table.

Purchase roses for gifts.

Charge your camera battery and ensure space is available on the memory card.

Day of Tea

Make cucumber sandwiches and fruit kabobs (or any other perishable menu item).

Set up serving trays with an assortment of treats.

Fill the coffee urn with water and have it heating throughout the morning.

Place tea bags in the urn approximately 15 minutes prior to guests arriving.

Sample Task Checklist

	Althea	Andreas	Anna	Aurora	Ben	Emma	Fionn	Foster	Innes	Lidia	Lila	Maia	Oliver	Paige	Piper	Toby
Paint Invitation	X		X		X		X		X		X		X		X	
Interview	X		X		X		X		X		X		X		X	
Dedication Page	X		X		X		X		X		X		X		X	
Photo	X		X		X		X		X		X		X		X	
Write in Card/Sign	X		X		X		X		X		X		X		X	
Place Card - M's Name	X		X		X		X		X		X		X		X	
Gift Tags	X		X		X		X		X		X		X		X	
Make pin	X		X		X		X		X		X		X		X	
Wrap pin	X		X		X		X		X		X		X		X	
Baking	X		X		X		X		X		X		X		X	
Guest face circles	X		X		X		X		X		X		X		X	
Guest squares	X		X		X		X		X		X		X		X	

Teacher Tasks:

1. print/send pre-invite
2. print teacup invitation — double-sided on card stock
3. make copies of interview sheet; type up interviews when complete
4. print dedication pages
5. print photos
6. make place cards — choose stamp
7. gift tags?
8. buy gift wrap
9. buy baking ingredients
10. cut out flower circles

Sample Schedule: Day of the Event

Children's Arrival at School until Teatime

8:15 – 10:00 A.M.
>
> Practice – greetings and taking orders
>
> Rehearse – entertainment
>
> Read – stories to keep the children engaged
>
> Go – encourage children to use the bathroom 30 minutes
> prior to guests arriving!
>
> Prepare – get ready for guests to arrive by sitting in chairs

Teatime 10:00 A.M.
>
> Teacher welcomes guests and invites them to enter the room one by one.
> It is wise to wait until all guests have arrived before beginning to invite
> them into the room. This
> ensures that each child will have a guest. It works well to fill the
> room from back to front.

10:10 – 10:15 A.M.
>
> Once children and guests have had time to greet each other and settle
> in to their chairs, signal the room that the tea will begin (turn lights on,
> ring chime/bell, play music, etc.).
>
> Children take orders, serve treats, eat and drink with guest.
>
> Volunteers take tea to guest at table and fill child's cup with lemonade/
> water or other beverage for children.
>
> Child can return to treat table as often as you designate – set limits or
> allow unlimited visits.
>
> During this period, designate someone to take photographs of the room,
> the guests, children, and the performance. Be sure to take at least one
> photo of each children with his/her guest. These photos can be displayed
> after the tea or used in newsletters or websites.

10:40 – 10:45 A.M.
>
> Invite children to the front of the room for their performance.

10:55 – 11:00 A.M.
>
> At the close of the performance, thank the guest for coming, and offer
> each child a flower to give to his/her guest as a farewell gift.

Our tea is over,

Our songs are all sung,

Goodbye,

Goodbye to everyone.

Goodbye to the cookies,

Goodbye to the tea,

Goodbye to you

and

Goodbye to me!

Afterword

Master Class Materials would like to thank Chris, Carl, Jim, Evan, and Emily for their help and support in making this book possible. If you would like additional copies of **Spring Tea** or view other titles published by Master Class Materials, please visit: **masterclassmaterials.com**

Made in the USA
Charleston, SC
20 May 2014